Praise for the Believe Series

"As grandparents of fifty grandchildren, we heartily endorse the *Believe . . . and You're There* series. Parents and grandparents, gather your children around you and discover the scriptures again as they come alive in the *Believe . . . and You're There* series."

—STEPHEN AND SANDRA COVEY
Stephen Covey is the bestselling author of *7 Habits of Highly Effective People*

"Bravo! This series is a treasure! You pray that your children will fall in love with and get lost in the scriptures just as they are discovering the wonder of reading. This series does it. Two thumbs way, way up!"

—MACK AND REBECCA WILBERG
Mack Wilberg is the music director of the Mormon Tabernacle Choir

"This series is a powerful tool for helping children learn to liken the scriptures to themselves. Helping children experience the scriptural stories from their point of view is genius."

—ED AND PATRICIA PINEGAR
Ed Pinegar is the bestselling author of *Raising the Bar*

"We only wish these wonderful books had been available when we were raising our own children. How we look forward to sharing them with all our grandchildren!"

—STEPHEN AND JANET ROBINSON
Stephen Robinson is the bestselling author of *Believing Christ*

"The *Believe . . . and You're There* series taps into the popular genre of fantasy and imagination in a wonderful way. Today's children will be drawn into the reality of events described in the scriptures. Ever true to the scriptural accounts, the authors have crafted delightful stories that will surely awaken children's vivid imaginations while teaching truths that will often sound familiar."

—TRUMAN AND ANN MADSEN
Truman Madsen is the bestselling author of *Joseph Smith, the Prophet*

"My dad and I read *At the Miracles of Jesus* together. First I'd read a chapter, and then he would. Now we're reading the next book. He says he feels the Spirit when we read. So do I."

—CASEY J., AGE 9

"My mom likes me to read before bed. I used to hate it, but the *Believe* books make reading fun and exciting. And they make you feel good inside, too."

—KADEN T., AGE 10

"Reading the *Believe* series with my tweens and my teens has been a big spiritual boost in our home—even for me! It always leaves me peaceful and more certain about what I believe."

—GLADYS A., AGE 43

"I love how Katie, Matthew, and Peter are connected to each other and to their grandma. These stories link children to their families, their ancestors, and on to the Savior. I heartily recommend them for any child, parent, or grandparent."

—ANNE S., AGE 50
Mother of ten, grandmother of nine (and counting)

When Lehi Left Jerusalem

Believe and You're There

When Lehi Left Jerusalem

Book 5

ALICE W. JOHNSON & ALLISON H. WARNER

DESERET
BOOK

Salt Lake City, Utah

In memory of Jerry Harston (1943–2009),
with deep gratitude

Text © 2010 Alice W. Johnson, Allison H. Warner

Illustrations © 2010 Jerry Harston

Library of Congress Cataloging-in-Publication Data
Johnson, Alice W.
    Believe and you're there when Lehi left Jerusalem / Alice W. Johnson and Allison H. Warner ; illustrated by Jerry Harston.
        p. cm.
    Summary: Through their Grandma's magical paintings, Katie, Matthew, and Peter travel to Jerusalem at the time of the prophet Lehi.
    ISBN 978-1-60641-246-6 (paperbound)
    1. Lehi (Book of Mormon figure)—Juvenile literature.   2. Book of Mormon stories.   I. Warner, Allison H.   II. Harston, Jerry.   III. Title.
    BX8627.4.L44J64 2010
    289.3'22—dc22   2009038544

Printed in the United States of America
R. R. Donnelley, Crawfordsville, IN

10   9   8   7   6   5   4   3   2   1

Believe in the wonder,
Believe if you dare,
Believe in your heart,
Just believe . . . and you're there!

Contents

Chapter One

Hot and Tired

"I'm tired of doing this! I am not pulling one more weed, no matter what you two say!" Peter hollered across Grandma's backyard to his two older siblings, Katie and Matthew. Then he plopped himself down under a thick, bushy shade tree. With his chin in his hands and his legs criss-crossed, Peter looked miserable.

At long last school was out, and summer vacation had begun. Even better, a long-promised weekend at Grandma's had finally arrived.

"Come on, Peter," Matthew called back. "There's not that much left to do!"

"No way! I am done with weeding!" Peter insisted.

"Well, the sooner we get it done, the sooner we can go to the cottage to see Grandma's new painting,"

Katie reminded him, hoping to entice Peter back to the job at hand.

"I don't care about the new painting right now," Peter moaned, without budging. "You two are the ones who agreed to do the weeding, not me."

Weeding Grandma's backyard was definitely not Peter's idea of fun. Actually, Matthew and Katie didn't really like it, either. But, when you got right down to it, they felt good when they helped Grandma.

More importantly, they couldn't wait to experience another one of Grandma's paintings. Her beautiful scripture scenes were so real, the children were transported right into the story. They couldn't wait to see what adventures awaited them this time. The promise of a new painting just inside the art cottage made Matthew and Katie work all the faster. But today, Peter simply was not cooperating.

"But you're doing such a good job!" Katie said sweetly to pouting Peter, hoping this different approach would get him working again.

"It's just too hot out here," was his stubborn reply, his chin still planted firmly in his hands.

Katie gave Matthew a pleading look. She needed his help.

"Hey, bud, I know it's hot. But at least we're all in this together." Matthew tried to sound upbeat.

Just as Peter started to give an angry reply, Grandma came around the corner of the house with a big pitcher of ice-cold lemonade and four glasses on a tray.

"Come and get some lemonade," she invited the children. Matthew and Katie put down their tools and ran to her. They grabbed the tall, icy glasses with their muddy hands.

Matthew gulped down his drink without coming up for air, and Grandma poured him another glass, full to the brim. Katie, on the other hand, sipped her drink slowly, savoring every refreshing mouthful. Peter sat hunched over under the nearby shade tree, frowning and muttering his frustration.

"What's the matter with Peter?" Grandma asked quietly. Katie and Matthew rolled their eyes and shook their heads.

"Well, it seems weeding isn't exactly his favorite activity," Katie answered with a wry smile.

"Tell him to join the club," Grandma chuckled. "Hey, Peter, come get some lemonade," she called cheerfully.

"No, thanks," Peter replied dejectedly. "I'm too tired."

"You?" Grandma sounded shocked. "You have more energy than anyone I know! How can you be too tired for lemonade?"

"Well, for one thing, I hate weeding! For another, I am too hot and tired to walk over to you. And for the last thing, I'm getting all dirty. And I don't like it!" He declared all this loudly and followed it with a noisy sigh.

"Oh, I see," Grandma said, suppressing a smile. "And I suppose Katie and Matthew just love to weed in the hot sun?"

Katie and Matthew started to protest. "We don't like weeding," they began, but Grandma held up her hand to shush them. Peter looked at Katie and Matthew as though he didn't believe them.

"You two really don't like weeding?" he asked. He turned to his grandma. "Well, how come they're so happy if they're doing something they don't like to do?" Peter demanded.

"That is a very interesting question," Grandma replied thoughtfully. "It looks to me like I have two Nephis and one Lemuel here today!"

"What do you mean?" Peter asked, his interest sparked.

Matthew took a stab at the answer. "In the Book of Mormon, Nephi was the one who believed his father, Lehi, and left Jerusalem to follow him into the desert."

"Oh, I get what you're trying to say," Peter said, the light going on in his head. "But wait! Lemuel went, too, you know."

"That's true, I guess," Katie agreed reluctantly. "But he and Laman complained all the way!"

"They probably had a lot to complain about," Peter grumbled.

Again, Matthew and Katie started to protest, and again, Grandma stopped them. "Let's think about this together," she said. "Peter, do you mind if I ask you a few questions?"

"Go ahead," he said.

"Okay, here's the first one. Did Nephi have to travel less far than Laman and Lemuel?"

"Hmmm." He thought for a minute. "No. I think they all traveled together."

Grandma went on, "Did Nephi have better food to eat on the journey than Laman and Lemuel did?"

Again Peter responded, "Probably not."

"Did Nephi get to travel in nicer weather than Laman and Lemuel?" Grandma asked.

"Of course not!" This time Peter had to chuckle as he answered.

"What about tents? Did they have the same kind of tents? And how about bugs . . ."

Peter stopped her. "Okay, okay, Grandma. I think I'm getting the picture."

"What picture is that, Peter dear?" Grandma asked innocently.

"Well . . . ," he ventured, "I think you are trying to say that even though they were all in it together, Laman and Lemuel chose to focus on the bad and complain, while Nephi chose to look at the good and be happy."

A smile started across Grandma's face as she nodded. "Do you think you're hotter than Katie and Matthew?"

"Probably not," he admitted.

"Are you more tired?"

He shook his head. "No."

"Do they like weeding more than you do?"

"NO!" Katie and Matthew practically shouted in unison.

"Are they less thirsty than you are?" she asked.

"Totally! They each had a big glass of lemonade, and I didn't!" By now, Peter couldn't help laughing out loud.

"Well, I can fix that in a flash." Grandma returned Peter's hearty laugh. She picked up the pitcher of cold lemonade, poured a big glass, and held it out for him. "Come and get it," she invited affectionately.

Peter jumped up and ran to grab the lemonade. "Thanks, Grandma! I really was thirsty. And thanks for the lesson. I think I get the big picture now."

"Speaking of big pictures, I have one right over there in the art cottage that I think you three will love!" Then she hesitated. "Um . . . it's . . . just that, um . . . there are still some weeds . . ."

"You don't have to ask me twice," Peter said, grabbing his shovel. "Just call me Nephi! I'm on it!" And off he went to attack the last few weeds, smiling from ear to ear.

Chapter Two

Same Place, Different Time

"Well, that didn't take long, did it?" Grandma observed as she stood outside the arched blue door of her art cottage. She surveyed her freshly weeded yard and flower beds. "This place looks beautiful, kids," she said gratefully. "Now, you all deserve a rest while I read to you about my new painting."

If this new painting was like the others—and it whisked all three children back in time to experience the scripture story it depicted—then they were in for anything but a rest! In fact, Katie, Matthew, and Peter thought there was nothing more exciting and adventurous than an encounter with one of Grandma's scripture paintings.

"What did you paint this time?" asked Katie, trying to sound nonchalant.

"Well, let's see if you can tell me," Grandma said.

"Hey, Grandma, can I be the one to start the password?" Peter interrupted.

"All right, Peter," Grandma agreed. "You be the gatekeeper today." She ceremoniously handed him the key. Taking his responsibility very seriously, Peter took his place just outside the locked entrance to the

magical world of Grandma's art cottage. Then Katie, Matthew, and Grandma lined up single file—Katie first, with Grandma bringing up the rear. Once everyone was in place, Peter nodded solemnly to Katie.

"Believe in the wonder," she began, chanting aloud the first line of the password.

"Believe if you dare," Matthew continued.

"Believe in your heart," Grandma said in turn.

"Just believe . . . and you're there!" They all finished the poem with gusto.

Then, with great anticipation, Peter turned the key in the lock, threw open the door with a flourish, and eagerly motioned for everyone to enter. They were greeted with the familiar smell of paint and a view of the large easel on which Grandma always placed her newest painting. And on the floor, right in front of the easel, were mounds of soft, inviting pillows beckoning the children to sit. Once in the cottage, Grandma stood next to the easel, which was covered, as usual, by a soft, white blanket. "Now, make yourselves comfortable, children," she instructed them, "and imagine that you're . . . HERE!"

Grandma whisked the blanket off the easel. And there it was—a painting of a crowded ancient city street that looked nothing like the quiet, suburban avenue where Grandma lived. This dusty street, thronged with animals and people, was lined with tents made of animal skins, and small, square adobe buildings with flat rooftops. Each roof seemed to be protected by another roof, as though the lower roof were a patio of sorts, with a rooflike canopy above it.

It all looked somewhat familiar to the children, who had traveled to old Jerusalem in Jesus' time through another painting of Grandma's.

But this city street looked more primitive than the Jerusalem they had visited earlier, except for one thing: above the busy city scene, in the distance and atop a gentle hill, sat a large, palatial home. Its light brown stucco walls were adorned with scrolling gold decorations. Grandma had painted the grounds around the house a lush green and they were surrounded by a stone wall. In the middle of the front section of the wall was an ornate wooden gate. Katie was the first to speak. "Someone rich must live in that house on the hill."

"Yes," observed Matthew. "The house is different, but the rest of the street looks kind of familiar."

"Yeah, I think I've been there before," Peter said, sounding a little disappointed.

"Really?" Grandma looked at him quizzically.

Katie and Matthew, sitting on either side of Peter, jabbed at him with their elbows.

"Well . . . ," Peter caught his mistake. "It just seems like I've been there because your paintings always look so real." Poor Peter was doing his best to recover from his blunder.

Katie joined in to help her bumbling brother.

"Your paintings are so good, Grandma, I always feel as though I am actually there. Peter probably feels the same way."

"Tell us about this one," Matthew encouraged Grandma, changing the subject.

Grandma smiled. "It's Jerusalem, but our story today is from the Book of Mormon, not the New Testament."

"Well, if it's from the Book of Mormon, why did you do a painting of Jerusalem?" Peter was puzzled. "Didn't Book of Mormon people live on the American continent?"

"Eventually, Peter," Grandma said, nodding her agreement. "But the Book of Mormon begins in Jerusalem, a long, long time before Jesus lived there."

"Well, how did all those people end up in America?" Peter persisted.

"I guess we'd better start at the beginning," Grandma said thoughtfully, as she sat down in the rocking chair. She picked up her worn copy of the Book of Mormon and perched her glasses on the end of her nose.

"The book that we know as the Book of Mormon was translated from gold plates by Joseph Smith," she began.

"Where did he get the plates?" Peter blurted out.

Matthew was impatient for the story to begin. "Just listen, buddy," he told his little brother, "and you'll get the whole story. Go on, Grandma."

"I'll try to make this quick," she assured Peter. "You remember Moroni from the Book of Mormon? He was the last prophet who wrote on the plates. They had been passed down from one prophet to another for more than a thousand years! Before he died, Moroni buried the gold plates in a hill. That was about one thousand six hundred years ago. Now this hill is in the state of New York in the United States of America, and it is called the Hill Cumorah. Young Joseph Smith lived in Palmyra, New York, not far from the hill. The angel Moroni, who is a resurrected being, appeared to Joseph and told him about the gold plates.

"As Moroni was talking, Joseph saw a vision in his mind that showed him where the plates were buried. The vision was so clear that Joseph recognized the place again when he visited it." Grandma took a deep breath.

"Keep going, Grandma. We're right with you," Matthew said encouragingly.

She continued, "Four years after Moroni first

visited, Joseph was finally allowed to take the plates from the Hill Cumorah to begin translating them."

"But how does Jerusalem fit into all of this?" Peter said, still sounding puzzled.

"Stay with me, Peter. We're almost there. The first story in the Book of Mormon is about a prophet named Lehi who lived with his family in Jerusalem."

"Finally!" Peter sounded relieved. "Now we're getting somewhere."

Grandma chuckled. "Matthew, I'll bet you can fill in some details from here."

"Let's see," Matthew began earnestly. "Lehi was a prophet of God. He was told in a vision that Jerusalem would be destroyed unless the people repented. But when he tried to warn people, they made fun of him. Some people even wanted to kill him."

"That's a perfect introduction to our story, Matthew. I know just where to begin reading. We'll start with the words of Lehi's son, Nephi." Grandma paused, took a deep breath, and began to read:

"'For behold, it came to pass that the Lord spake unto my father, yea, even in a dream, and said unto him: Blessed art thou Lehi, because of the things which thou hast done. . . .'"

Chapter Three

Up, Up, and Away

The moment Grandma started reading, the tiny figures in the painting came alive, bustling along the narrow streets of Jerusalem.

A wide smile flashed on Peter's face, his eyes sparkling with anticipation. "Look, you guys," he whispered, pointing to the tiny, moving people. "Let's go!"

"Do you think it's safe?" Matthew whispered back. "After all, those people want to kill Lehi."

"Yeah, but we're not Lehi. And nobody knows who we are," Peter responded.

"That's true," Matthew nodded, mouthing his agreement. Cautious Matthew, unlike impulsive Peter, liked to see a situation from every angle.

"Shall we go?" Katie whispered. Peter and

Matthew both signaled their readiness with a smile and a nod, and Katie offered each brother a hand.

They paused for a moment, their hands grasped tightly together, and studied the painting expectantly. Katie took a good look at Grandma who read on, seemingly unaware of the adventure about to unfold. Peter, with a twinkle in his eye and a hand poised to launch them into the painting, looked like a basketball player waiting for the tip-off. Finally, when Katie was satisfied that all was in order, she winked meaningfully at Peter, and he plunged his hand into the canvas.

As his hand disappeared from view, rushing wind enveloped the children, lifting them up and away from the quiet cottage. "Yahoo!" Peter exclaimed, as the siblings were propelled toward ancient Jerusalem and another memorable scripture adventure. Katie's blonde ponytail billowed behind her in the wind, and she tried to enjoy the ride as much as her enthusiastic little brother.

"Look," Peter cried. "You can see the city now!"

As Matthew felt the slowing descent of the journey's end, a ripple of excitement passed through his body. Jerusalem really was an amazing place, he thought. And now they were going to see what it was like six hundred years before Jesus was born!

The swirling air began to subside, and the children landed gently just outside the busy city gates of Jerusalem. Even outside the city wall, the children sensed that Jerusalem was much smaller than when they had visited before. The Temple of Solomon still dominated the elevated center of the city, and worshippers were streaming up to the temple mount with goats and lambs in tow to sacrifice. Matthew guessed that Jerusalem's surrounding walls were only about fifteen feet tall (much shorter than in Jesus' time), and the marketplace just outside the city gates was not nearly as crowded.

"There aren't as many people here as there were last time," Matthew said, sounding thoughtful. "It wouldn't take much to stick out here. Peter, that means you can't just go running off on your own," he cautioned.

"Right," Katie had the very same concern. "Let's stick together, okay, Peter?"

"Agreed!" Peter responded with a hearty salute. "But," he quickly added with a grumble, "these clothes are going to drive me crazy. They are even itchier than the last time we were here!"

"They are pretty scratchy," Katie concurred, "and I wish mine weren't boring brown."

"Well, since this is all we have, let's try to make the best of it," Matthew suggested, trying to sound cheerful.

In the heart of the marketplace, where the children found themselves, the atmosphere was charged with excitement and action. Merchants who had come to trade food and merchandise had erected tents and stalls at every turn.

The children were fascinated by the unfamiliar way people bought and sold things.

"Men's sturdy sandals for six loaves!" shouted one man, standing before a small tent displaying leather goods.

"Three warm shawls for a barrel of wine! Two shawls for a flask of fish oil!" called a young boy, gesturing to a cart piled with heavy gray fabrics.

When someone was interested in what was offered, he approached the merchant to strike a deal. After a friendly exchange that began with "shalom," a hearty handshake, and a pat on the shoulder, the bargaining began in earnest.

"Nobody seems to be buying things with money." Matthew was perplexed. "Everyone hollers about what they've got and what they need, until two people who each have what the other wants find each other. And then they have to work out who will give how much."

"It's quite a system, isn't it?" marveled Katie. "There's a lot of yelling, but it all seems to work just fine. Crazy, isn't it, Peter . . . Peter? Peter!" But he was gone.

How could it be? Katie's heart leapt into her throat as she wheeled around, trying to spot her youngest brother. Wasn't it just two minutes ago that she had warned him about staying together? And now he was nowhere to be found!

"Where did he go?" Katie frantically demanded of Matthew.

"How would I know?" Poor Matthew sounded both frustrated and worried. But when he saw the tears starting to well up in Katie's eyes, he tried to reassure her. "He'll show up, Sis. He always does." But Matthew's heart was pounding, too.

The children scanned the merchants' stands for some sign of Peter. Holding hands, they weaved quickly in and out of the busy crowds. At last they spotted him. Leaning over a stand laden with fruits, nuts, and olives, Peter was confidently inspecting the items like an expert. He seemed not to have a care in the world.

Katie and Matthew nearly cried with relief as they barreled toward their little brother.

"Peter! Peter! There you are!" Matthew hollered.

Peter waved a cheery greeting. "Shalom. That's how they say 'hello' around here," he explained, completely oblivious to the fact that Katie and Matthew were beside themselves with worry.

"That's wonderful," Matthew said, trying to keep his voice even, "but why did you go off by yourself?"

"I was hungry, and I saw this food over here," Peter replied matter-of-factly.

"And how were you going to pay for it?" Katie, like Matthew, did her best to regain her composure.

"Well, that's the problem. I don't have anything to trade for it," Peter said, explaining his dilemma.

Just then, the merchant selling the food on display approached the children. "Shalom," he greeted them kindly.

"Uh . . . shalom," Matthew replied tentatively.

"I haven't seen you before around here. You must be here for the upcoming festival. There are so many visitors in town," the merchant told them.

"Yes, we're visitors here," Matthew responded. "What kind of cheese is that?" he added, quickly changing the subject.

"It is goat cheese, and this is a very good batch. Would you like some?" he asked, holding it up for them to see.

"What would you take for it?" Katie asked, taking off her small silver earrings. "Would these do?"

"Those would do nicely, but let me add some grapes and almonds, too," the merchant said as he deposited a generous help- ing of each into their out- stretched palms.

"Thank you very much," the hungry chil- dren said gratefully, as they sat down on the low rock wall next to the food stall. They quickly divided up the food and began to eat.

"Delicious!" Matthew exclaimed, as he bit into a large grape, sending a juicy blast into his mouth and quenching his thirst.

"What's your name?" friendly Peter asked the merchant.

The merchant laughed, surprised by Peter's forthright way. "I am called Darius," he answered. "And you are called . . . ?"

"I'm Peter, and this is my sister, Katie, and my brother, Matthew," Peter said.

"I see. Shalom to all of you. Are you staying in the city?" Darius inquired.

"Uh, we're not sure," Matthew replied, unsure of what to say. "We don't have a place to stay yet."

"Well, the city is filling up quickly. It is doubtful that you will find anywhere now. Why don't you stay with my family and me?" Darius offered.

"Father, Father!" A boy and girl about the ages of Matthew and Katie called out to Darius as they hurried toward him.

Darius's eyes filled with delight as he embraced his two children. "Aaron! Leah! Come meet my new friends. Peter, Katie, and Matthew, these are my children, Aaron and Leah."

"Shalom!" Aaron and Leah were outgoing and friendly.

"Shalom." The three children from another time tried to say the unfamiliar word with confidence, as if greeting people this way was something they did every day.

"I have invited Matthew, Peter, and Katie to stay with us, children, because the city is so full for the festival," Darius told his children. "Why don't you take them home to meet Mother? I will return when business is finished for the day."

"Father," Aaron spoke as if he had important news. "We came to tell you that Laban's head servant wants the big festival order delivered to Laban's house this afternoon."

"Wonderful! That is a day earlier than I expected," Darius said happily. "They must be preparing for the festival like everyone else." Whenever there was a festival, business was especially good, and that made Darius smile. It wasn't always easy to provide well for his family selling fruits and nuts and cheese, so Darius was always glad to profit from extra business whenever it was time for a traditional Jewish celebration.

Matthew, Katie, and Peter followed Aaron and Leah away from the marketplace, and through the narrow, winding Jerusalem streets. In sharp contrast to the noisy chatter of business, these inner city lanes and alleys were quiet and calm.

"Now we can talk," Aaron said as he walked with his new friends. "It is difficult even to hear yourself think at the market!"

"Will your mother mind if we come home with you with no warning?" Katie asked Leah.

"Not at all," Leah assured her. "She is accustomed to it. My father always brings visitors home when there is a festival. Aaron and I are especially glad this time that our visitors are close to our age."

"Hey!" Peter suddenly remembered Grandma's story. "Have you heard of a prophet named Lehi?"

Aaron and Leah stopped walking and stared at Peter. "Please, do not speak another word," Leah pleaded in a whisper. She and Aaron looked positively frightened.

"Did I say something wrong?" Peter asked.

"Shhh." Aaron put his finger to his lips. "We will be home soon."

Chapter Four

Of Sinners and Hypocrites

The children hurried along in worried silence. Stopping at a rough wooden door, Aaron lifted its latch and opened it inward, revealing a small earthen courtyard.

"What did I say that made everyone nervous?" Peter asked, when the gate was safely closed behind the children.

"In Jerusalem these days, Peter, you must be very careful what you say about the prophets and where you say it," Aaron replied.

"Has Lehi done something wrong?" Matthew asked anxiously.

"No, he has not done anything wrong," Leah assured him. "He has only tried to warn the people of Jerusalem to repent."

"Why do they need to repent?" Katie asked.

"Many people here are no longer obeying the commandments that God gave to Moses for us to follow," Aaron told her.

"But wasn't that a long time ago?" Matthew asked.

"Yes, it was, but it is still the word of God," Aaron said soberly.

"That is very true," Matthew agreed.

"When you say 'not obeying the commandments,' does that mean people are stealing?" Peter asked.

"Yes," Aaron responded.

"And worshiping idols?" Peter went on.

"Yes."

"And," Peter took a deep breath, "even . . . even murdering people?" Peter closed his eyes after this question, not sure he wanted to hear the answer.

"I'm afraid so," said Aaron sadly.

Peter was stunned. "That is totally wrong! Why doesn't somebody do something about it?"

"That is exactly what Lehi was trying to do," Leah said. "But after he told people they should repent and follow God, they wanted to kill him."

"Kill him just for telling the truth?" Matthew was incredulous.

"People don't like to be told they're doing the wrong thing, especially when they are," Katie pointed out to her brother. "Usually it just makes them mad."

"Was Lehi the only one telling the truth?" Matthew asked Aaron.

"No, there is another prophet who has tried to warn the people, just as Lehi has been doing. His name is Jeremiah," Aaron told him.

"But they haven't killed him, have they?" Matthew asked.

"Well, the people have not killed him, but he has been put in prison. Some leaders don't like his teachings any more than the people do," Leah responded.

"What about Lehi? What is he going to do?" Matthew asked, clearly concerned.

"Lehi has taken his family and left the city. None of his family has been seen for many days," Aaron said. "We all wonder where they have gone."

"Well, if people wanted to kill me, I wouldn't stick around either," Peter announced. "If you ask me, Lehi sounds like a pretty smart man."

"He is not just a smart man, Peter. He is a prophet," Aaron said, remembering the strong feelings he had whenever he heard Lehi preach. He knew in his heart that Lehi was a true prophet of God.

"There must be some people who believe Lehi and Jeremiah. Is everyone in Jerusalem against them?" Katie wondered.

"No, not everyone. But most people in Jerusalem are not valiant for the truth. We cannot trust our neighbors or our friends. That is why I became frightened when Peter asked about Lehi while we were still in the streets. I was worried that the wrong people would hear us say that we believed Lehi, and then things would become hard for my family," Aaron explained.

"Could I ask a question?" Katie interjected. "If everyone is so wicked, why did we see so many people going to the temple to offer sacrifices?"

"That is perhaps the worst of it," Leah lamented. "People go to the temple to worship and perform sacrificial rites. They act as if they are living the commandments, and then they turn around and do sinful things. They are hypocrites," she finished, sounding discouraged.

"Hippo . . . what?" Peter blurted out. "I didn't know they had hippos in Jerusalem."

"Not that kind of a hippo," Matthew replied, smiling. "A hypocrite is someone who claims to believe one thing but does something different. Let me think of an example . . ."

Katie leaned over and whispered in Matthew's ear. Matthew looked at her with his mouth wide open, as if he were shocked. Then he relaxed.

"Okay, Katie," he relented good-naturedly. "I'll admit you're probably right. Peter, here's an example of a hypocrite: I'm a bit of a hypocrite when I tell you that it's really important to make your bed every morning—and then I don't always do it myself."

"Well, until we are all perfect, I am sure we are all hypocrites sometimes," Aaron assured Matthew. "But at least we are trying to do what is right."

"Aaron, Leah," a gentle voice called from inside the house.

"We are out here, Mother," Leah called back.

"I have been waiting for you to make that large delivery to Laban's house. They are going to need it soon." Their mother appeared in the doorway. "Oh, you have brought some friends home, I see," she said, smiling at the unfamiliar children.

"Yes, Mother. They are here for the festival. We met them at Father's stand. They have no place to stay tonight, so Father invited them to stay with us," Aaron told her. "This is Katie, and these are her brothers, Matthew and Peter."

"Welcome," she greeted them warmly. "We are happy to have you as our guests. My name is Deborah. Perhaps you would be willing to help Aaron and Leah with their delivery."

"We sure would!" Peter was enthusiastic, as usual.

"Wonderful!" Deborah exclaimed. "Aaron, get the cart and we'll get you on your way."

"Come, Matthew and Peter. I could use some help with the cart," Aaron said, beckoning the boys and disappearing around the corner of the house. Matthew and Peter followed, waving happily to Katie and Leah as they ran to catch up.

Chapter Five

A Walk through Old Jerusalem

Matthew and Aaron pulled a large wooden cart around the side of the house, bringing it to a stop in the small courtyard. Katie, Leah, and Deborah appeared at the front door, laden with woven sacks filled with food for Laban's household. After they had placed the sacks near the cart, they returned to the house for more.

"Boy, oh boy. These are really heavy," Peter groaned as he hoisted sacks filled with almonds, figs, pomegranates, and large bricks of cheese onto the cart.

"That sure is a lot of food," Matthew said to Aaron when they had loaded the last sack. "Where did it all come from?"

"My father's family has a farm outside the city. They raise livestock there, and they grow a lot of different crops," Aaron explained. "Father brings the crops and cheeses to the city, and then he sells them from his stand outside the city gates, where you met him earlier today."

"Here is some fresh cheese for you to share on your way to Laban's house," Deborah said, handing them a small yellow brick. "Hurry now, children. Laban likes his deliveries on time."

"Matthew, give me a hand up here," Aaron said, motioning to Matthew to grab one side of the cart's handle. "Peter, if you push from the back, and we pull from the front, this shouldn't be hard at all."

"Yes, sir!" Peter saluted Aaron enthusiastically, and he hurried to his post behind the cart. Leah unlatched the gate and pulled it open. Pushing and pulling, the three boys guided the wooden cart down the dirt-packed lane, with the girls on either side. The procession made its way slowly along. Darius's awkward cart (which was considered one of the finest in Jerusalem) rode on clumsy wooden wheels, making for a very bumpy ride. Matthew silently reflected on the blessing of latter-day rubber tires. The girls kept an eye on the contents of the cart as the delivery sacks bobbed up and down, up and down. The children chatted with each other and munched happily on chunks of warm cheese as they moved through the city.

"How far is it to Laban's house?" Katie asked.

"It is in another quarter of the city, but it shouldn't take us long. And besides, we will be able to show you the temple and the king's palace on the way," Leah told her.

"And," Aaron added in a low voice, "we will also go right by Lehi's house. I will point it out when we get there, but please do not say anything about it until we are safely home again."

"You can trust us," Matthew replied seriously, turning his head to give Peter a meaningful look.

"Who is this Laban that we're taking food to?" Peter asked Aaron.

Aaron looked around to make sure that no one was close enough to eavesdrop, and then he answered in a quiet voice, "Laban is a very powerful man here in Jerusalem. He controls the treasury, he commands fifty soldiers, and he meets often with Jewish leaders." The children could tell by the way Aaron talked that he did not think well of Laban.

"What's a treasury?" Matthew wanted to know.

Aaron answered, "You know, where gold and silver and other riches are kept."

"Oh," Matthew said out loud. And then to himself

he added, "Sounds kind of like the ancient version of a bank."

Leah continued telling about Laban. "Laban is cruel and short-tempered. I am always glad if he is not at home when we make a delivery."

"Let's hope he's not there today. I don't think I want to meet him," Katie told Leah.

"There is the Temple Mount," Aaron interrupted as they rounded a corner and the temple came into view. "The temple is the building with the large bronze pillars on either side of the front door."

"And that is the king's palace right next to the temple," Leah pointed out.

"It is beautiful," Katie said, stopping to take it all in.

"We better keep going," Aaron urged everyone. "We'll stop on our way back if you like, but first, we must quickly get these things over to Laban's house."

With Peter pushing, and Matthew and Aaron pulling, the cart bounced again along the dusty road. The houses in this part of the city were much larger than in the area where Aaron and Leah lived. In the lush courtyards, servants busily drew water, swept, and prepared food.

One of the large homes they passed seemed

strangely quiet. The gate had been left slightly ajar and there were no servants scurrying about.

Aaron paused and looked carefully around to make sure they were alone. "This is Lehi's city house. He also has a home and some land outside the city, which were his inheritance. They are deserted, too," he said quietly.

The children peered into the empty courtyard. "They just disappeared and left all this behind?" Matthew whispered. Aaron nodded.

"Hey, what are you doing here?" The breath went out of Matthew as a large hand clamped down on his shoulder. He tried to say something but the words got stuck in his throat. All that came out was a strange squeaking noise. He looked to Aaron, his eyes pleading for help.

"We are going to Laban's house to make a food delivery," Aaron bravely announced to the two gruff men who seemed to have appeared from nowhere. One was tall and lean, and the other—the one gripping Matthew's shoulder—was shorter and very muscular.

Katie and Leah hid behind the cart. "Do you know Laman and Lemuel, the sons of Lehi, who lived in this house?" the tall one demanded.

"Only by sight," Aaron replied.

"Their father is crazy. He thinks he is a prophet, and that Jerusalem is going to be destroyed. Supposedly he had a vision from God!" the man went on, mocking Lehi's claims. "If you ask me, it is all the imagination of a mad man!"

"He says Jerusalem will be destroyed because it is wicked," the short one added scornfully. "Hah! Nothing can harm a city as powerful as Jerusalem!"

"And then there's Nephi, the youngest son. He thinks he is so much better than everyone else," the tall one sneered angrily. "He agrees with his father, just to get on his good side. Lehi should listen to Laman and Lemuel, the only smart ones in that family. Besides, they are the oldest sons. They deserve a little respect!"

"Aaron, Matthew," a familiar voice called out.

"Father!" Aaron turned to see Darius approaching them. A wave of relief passed through all the children.

Katie and Leah ventured out from behind the cart and edged toward Darius for protection. Peter popped up from between the sacks in the cart where he was hiding, got a good look at the two rough-looking men, and ducked right back down again. Darius stood between the children and the men.

"I see you have met my children," he said to the strange men.

"Yes, but they were no help at all." The tall one sounded annoyed. "We are looking for Laman and Lemuel."

"I see," Darius replied. "Well, if you would please excuse us, we must be on our way. Good luck finding your friends."

"It is no use. They are probably gone for good," the short man grumbled.

Darius hurried to catch up with the children, who had wasted no time putting some distance between themselves and the frightening men. The girls struggled to push the cart from behind, as it was now extra-heavy with a scared stowaway onboard. As Darius joined the group, Peter jumped up and clambered out of the cart.

"Father, I am so grateful you found us." Leah was almost tearful as she spoke.

"Did those men hurt any of you?" Darius asked, looking the children over.

"No, but they gave me an awful feeling inside," Aaron replied.

"Yes, they are just like Laman and Lemuel. I've encountered them and their group of friends many times at the market. I never like to have them come around my stall, because they are all disrespectful and arrogant," he told the children.

"They sure don't like Nephi much, and they think Lehi is crazy," Matthew told Darius.

"Many people today don't believe what the prophets say. They have strayed so far from the truth, they cannot tell right from wrong anymore. But this I know, children: There is, indeed, a God, and we will be happy only if we follow His laws." Darius spoke with quiet authority and power.

"How did you come to feel that way?" Katie asked.

"I heard the prophets speak, and I wanted to know if what they said was true. I prayed and asked God to tell me. He visited me here," Darius put his hand to his chest. "And now I believe all the words the prophets have spoken."

"I want to feel that way, too," Matthew said earnestly.

"You can," Darius promised the boy. "Anyone can. If you truly want to know, ask God in faith. He will soften your heart, and you, too, will believe."

Matthew looked into Darius's eyes and felt the strength of his testimony as he spoke. Tonight, he told himself, I will pray, just as Darius did. I want to know for myself that the words of the prophets are true.

Chapter Six

Nephi's Courage

"Okay, children. Those unkind men are long gone, so let us hurry. Laban's household will be expecting this delivery," Darius said as he encouraged the children.

Their encounter with the friends of Laman and Lemuel had been upsetting, but all the children felt safer now with Darius accompanying them to Laban's house.

The group turned at the end of a lane, and a quiet, lovely road opened before them, sloping upward, and ending with a large gated home perched on top of the knoll the children were now ascending. Katie, Matthew, and Peter gasped. They were looking directly up at the ornate house in Grandma's painting, and it was Laban's house!

Matthew turned toward Katie and said quietly,

"Well, Sis, you said that house must belong to someone rich. It looks like you were exactly right."

As they neared the gate to the beautiful grounds
surrounding the home, Aaron and Matthew slowed
the cart and guided it to a stop. Inside the courtyard,
an angry scuffle could be heard, and then a threaten-
ing voice shouted out above the rest, "Thou art a
robber, and I will slay thee." Without warning, the
front gate flew open, and a young man was violently
thrust into the street. The gate slammed shut behind

him. Stunned, Darius and the children ducked quickly behind the cart.

"I told you I hated to come when Laban was here," Leah muttered quietly.

"Was that Laban yelling?" Katie asked, cowering nervously with Leah.

"It certainly was. I recognized that voice right away," Leah replied.

Crouched behind the cart, they watched the young man in the street rise slowly to his feet. Three

other young men hurried around the corner to assist him.

Darius watched wide-eyed. "Those are the sons of Lehi," he whispered in amazement. "They left the city with their father. It is dangerous for them to be back here."

"Why would they come back?" Aaron asked his father.

"I have no idea," Darius answered his son. "Laman is the one who was thrown out by Laban. The angry one on the right is Lemuel. The next one is Sam, and the tall, strong one is Nephi, the youngest."

"Laman, are you all right?" Lemuel asked his brother.

"Does it look like I am all right?" Laman shot back at his brother, brushing the dust from his clothes. Then, turning on Nephi, he said, "I told you and Father that this was a hard thing he required of us, but you two wouldn't listen to me."

"Yes," replied Nephi patiently, but with confidence, "it is hard. But it is not Father who required it of us. It is the Lord."

"Please!" Laman exploded in disgust. "Father is a

visionary man. He says God tells him what to do, but how do we know he is telling the truth?"

"I know he is telling the truth," Nephi answered firmly in his father's defense. "As the Lord liveth, and as we live, we will not go down unto our father in the wilderness until we have accomplished the thing which the Lord has commanded us."

"I say we go back right now," Lemuel said, facing off against Nephi.

Nephi stood even taller, and spoke to his older brothers with clarity and courage. "Let us be faithful in keeping the commandments of the Lord. Let us go down to the land of our father's inheritance, for he left behind gold and silver, and all manner of riches. We will take those riches and offer them to Laban in exchange for the records."

Lemuel scoffed, and then with his hands on his hips he demanded of Nephi, "What need do we have for the record engraven on the plates?"

Nephi replied with conviction, "The genealogy of our forefathers and the record of the Jews are on those plates. Wicked Jerusalem will be destroyed, and the records will be lost if we do not take them with us."

"Oh, all that crazy talk about Jerusalem being so

wicked! How could this great city ever be destroyed?" Laman scoffed defiantly.

"Brothers, it has been prophesied by God's servants," Nephi said simply. "We must obtain these plates to preserve the language of our fathers for our children and to remember the words which have been spoken by the holy prophets since the world began."

Laman's anger relaxed for a moment. But he quickly resumed his look of disgust, rolling his eyes at Lemuel as he spoke, "All right, Nephi. We will try this. But if this doesn't work, we are done trying, do you hear me?"

"Come then," Nephi spoke with determination. "Let us go quickly." And the four sons of Lehi turned and disappeared down the street.

"Boy, those two older brothers scare me to death," Katie whispered.

"Yeah," said Peter, almost to himself. "Maybe I grumbled about the weeding, but those guys aren't just whiners, they're downright mean!"

"They certainly are," Aaron agreed

"But it doesn't seem to change Nephi. He is loyal to his father and to God, even when it's hard. That takes courage," Matthew said with admiration.

"Let's make this delivery to Laban's steward, children. He is probably wondering where it is. Come." Darius picked up the handle of the cart and wheeled it to a smaller side gate a few yards away.

Upon entering, Darius instructed the children to unload the food onto wooden shelves just outside the servants' entrance to Laban's home. As they worked, Laban's steward approached them. He seemed flustered and worried.

"At last! I expected you earlier. Where have you been?"

"Forgive us," Darius explained apologetically. "There are extra demands on us because of the festival."

The steward was unmoved. "Laban expects us to have his table set just the same as always. And the entire household is in an uproar because Lehi's son, Laman, asked for the records that are in Laban's keeping! Laban flew into a rage and threatened to kill Laman. When Laban is angry, we all suffer."

Darius could see that the steward was afraid of Laban, and his heart went out to him. "Please forgive us if we have contributed to your hardship. It was not our intention. Is there anything we can do to help?"

The steward was caught off guard. He was not accustomed to being treated with respect and kindness, and he began to soften as Darius spoke.

"Actually, there is a way you might help," he began gratefully. "We are in need of even more provisions than I ordered. Laban has invited more guests than he originally planned, and I am going to come up short. Do you have more fruit and cheese you might bring for our evening meal?"

"Yes, I believe we do," Darius answered. "We will go as quickly as we can and return shortly. Come, children." Aaron and Leah fell in behind Darius who led the way, leaving Katie, Matthew, and Peter to bring up the rear.

As they hurried back through the narrow streets of Jerusalem, they talked about the events they had witnessed.

"Those records must be pretty important for Nephi to go to so much trouble to get them," Matthew observed.

"Yes, Matthew," Darius agreed. "Records are vital, for they help us remember the things God has revealed—to us and to our ancestors. And records help future generations learn from our mistakes and our successes. If we didn't keep records, our lives wouldn't mean much to the descendants that follow us."

"Hey! He's right!" Peter said to Katie and Matthew, as they followed Darius and his children. "I've done lots of interesting things in my life. How will my kids and grandkids know about them if I don't write them down?"

Katie smiled, thinking of all their scripture adventures. "That must be the reason that Grandma gave us those journals," she told her brothers. "She obviously knows something about keeping records that we don't."

"I want anyone who reads my journal to know exactly how I felt about the important things that happened to me," Matthew said.

"Yeah," Peter exclaimed, as though he had made an important discovery. "That way people can know me, even if they never met me!"

"And I want them to know the real me, right from my own mouth—or right from my own pen, I guess I should say," Matthew said, thinking out loud. And as they continued their hurried journey, Matthew's mind overflowed with thoughts and ideas that he couldn't wait to record in his journal.

Chapter Seven

If at First You Don't Succeed . . .

"I'm getting to know Jerusalem really well," Peter bragged, as once again the five children and Darius traveled through the city to Laban's house. "We're not far away now, are we?"

It was almost dusk, and as the sun dipped lower in the sky, the city had a peaceful, golden glow. Residents of Jerusalem hurried to their homes to join their families for the evening meal. Children who had been playing happily in the streets bid farewell to their friends, answering the calls of their mothers.

"Look, children! Laban's house is just at the top of this rise," Darius said, leading the small caravan up the hill. "On the way home, you can each take a turn riding on the cart. I think you have all earned a rest."

"Good!" Peter said with a dramatic sigh. "I've had just about enough walking for one day!"

While still a good distance from the house, the children noticed a group of four men ahead of them, approaching Laban's front gate with two large, full carts. Katie thought there was something familiar about the men, although they were still too far away to see their faces clearly. Then it came to her. "Leah, that's Nephi and his brothers, isn't it?"

"Oh my, it is!" Leah sounded shocked and scared at the same time.

Then Peter had the same realization. "Hey, that's . . ." he started, pointing up the street.

"Shhh! We know!" Matthew whispered to Peter. "They must have brought their expensive things like Nephi suggested."

"They surely are having a hard time getting those records," Aaron said.

"I am amazed at Nephi's courage. He is taking a big chance going back to Laban's house again," Matthew marveled.

"I think he is taking a big chance just hanging around those brothers of his!" Peter clearly didn't think much of Laman and Lemuel.

Darius listened to the children's observations and

then offered one of his own. "It is not just that Nephi has great courage," he began, "he must truly believe that when the Lord gives a commandment, He will make a way for it to be accomplished. That is what I call faith!"

"Look," Leah interrupted, "they are going into Laban's house!" And, indeed, Nephi and his brothers entered the gates and disappeared.

The steward appeared from the side gate. "Shalom," he greeted them. "Thank you for returning so soon. Things will be much easier for me because you brought these extra provisions. May your family be blessed for your kindness to me, which I do not deserve."

"Shalom," Darius responded with a friendly pat on the steward's back. "Please do not worry about what was said earlier. I can see that working for Laban must be very stressful. I am glad we could be of help. My name is Darius."

"Darius, I am indeed indebted to you. My name is Benjamin."

"Benjamin, I am pleased to know your name. Shall we take this food into the kitchen for you?"

"Please, come right in," Benjamin said gratefully, as he led the group through the back corridor into a large area where servants were preparing the evening meal for Laban's guests. With a stone floor and a large fire pit in its center, this room bore little resemblance to the gleaming kitchen with smooth counters, a refrigerator, and an electric stove where Katie, Matthew, and Peter's family prepared food.

"I noticed the sons of Lehi at your front gate when we approached," Darius said to Benjamin, as they deposited the food in the kitchen. "I thought the whole family had left Jerusalem for good when people threatened to kill Lehi."

"I thought so too, Darius. But it seems Lehi sent his sons back to retrieve the Jewish records in Laban's possession. That has really made Laban furious. Earlier today he refused to give up the records, and then he threw one of the brothers out into the street. I am surprised they have returned—and I guarantee that Laban won't be happy about it."

"The records on those plates must be very important or Lehi would not have sent his sons back to get them," Darius replied.

"Yes, I suppose so, but they don't seem so important to Laban. He does not live by the teachings of the prophets. I do not understand why he wants so badly to keep their writings."

Just at that moment, a terrified young servant boy (not much older than Katie) scurried through the door from Laban's private quarters. "Watch out," the servant warned Benjamin. "Lehi's sons have come back with their family treasures. They proposed a trade to Laban for the records. Laban agreed to the deal and called Zoram to open the treasury. Zoram put all of Lehi's silver and gold in there. Laban said he'd send a servant out with the plates, but he really has no intention of doing that. He is going to have the guards run those brothers off again, and he will keep all their gold and silver. I just hope that is all he does . . ."

The frightened servant seemed genuinely concerned about the safety of Nephi and his brothers. "You mustn't worry so," Benjamin said, trying to calm the young boy. "Laban is difficult, to be sure, but this trouble about the records will blow over soon, I am certain."

Just as Benjamin finished these consoling words, a loud, bellowing voice was heard from behind the door to Laban's chambers. "Kill them! Kill them all! I want you to find them and make sure none of them returns, ever!"

The young servant put his face in his hands and

shuddered. "I pray those four brothers remain safe," he moaned. Benjamin put his arm around the servant's shoulders. Then, remembering the presence of Darius and the children, he looked up with a start.

"You must go quickly," he urged them. "You do not want to be in this house when Laban is like this. Hurry! Hurry!" And Benjamin hastily ushered Darius and the children out of the kitchen, into the courtyard, and safely through the side gate.

"Whoa, that was scary!" Peter said, the gate slamming shut behind them.

As they hurried down the hill, they could still hear the clanging and clattering of servants rushing through the house, trying to satisfy Laban's impossible demands.

"Well, you have all worked very hard today," Darius said to the children, trying to take their minds off of their narrow escape. "When we get home, Mother will have dinner ready, and we can all eat and rest."

"I hope we get something more than nuts and fruit," Peter said under his breath to Matthew. "I can hardly wait to get home and have a big, juicy cheeseburger!"

"No kidding! And some french fries, too," Matthew said as his mouth began to water.

"Let's not talk about it anymore," Peter replied, holding his growling stomach.

"What is Nephi going to do now?" Katie wondered aloud to Leah. "It seemed really important to him to get those records."

"Yes, otherwise why would he have gone to all the trouble to get all their family's gold and silver and offer it to Laban in exchange?" Leah answered.

"I'll bet when Laban saw all their riches, he just decided to keep everything," Peter chimed in. "So he made a deal. They gave him their gold and silver, but he kept the plates. I'd say he's a pretty clever guy."

"Pretty mean, too!" Katie shuddered, glad to be away from Laban's house.

"Let's not talk of Laban anymore," Leah pleaded. "Let's think about something happy."

"I know what made me happy today." Katie spoke right up. "It was getting to know all of you!" And with that, she took Leah's hand, and together they skipped along the streets toward home.

Chapter Eight

The Lord Provides a Way

The next morning, Matthew was the first to wake up on the covered rooftop at Aaron and Leah's house. The sun shining over the hills surrounding Jerusalem warmed him, and he lay there perfectly content, listening to songbirds welcome the new day. Below, Jerusalem was coming to life. Women drew water from wells, men prepared for their labors, and sleepy children stirred, hungry for the morning meal.

Matthew reviewed in his mind all that had happened the previous day. He thought of meeting Darius, Aaron, and Leah—a very happy thought. He thought of Nephi and his brothers, and he couldn't help wondering what they would do now—a worried thought. And he thought of Laban, enraged by the request of Lehi's sons. Matthew was very glad he was nowhere near Laban's house this morning—a grateful thought.

One nagging concern kept running through Matthew's head. He nudged Katie, sleeping next to him. "Shhh," he cautioned her, as she opened first one eye and then the other. "Hey, Sis, I've been thinking: How much longer should we stay here? I'm afraid people are going to start asking questions we won't be able to answer very well."

"I was thinking the same thing last night," Katie replied, agreeing with her brother. "Let's find a good time to leave today. I'm sure going to miss Leah. She has become a good friend."

"I know what you mean," Matthew concurred. "It seems like I've known Aaron for a long, long time." As he spoke, he wistfully looked out over Jerusalem, a city he had grown to love.

"Children," Darius called from the courtyard below, "Mother has prepared breakfast. Please come down and eat."

"I'm sure hungry this morning!" Peter announced. "Let's go, sleepyheads!" and he jumped right up. In a flash, he shimmied down the ladder, landing in the courtyard below and leaving the other children peering down from the roof.

"Does Peter always move so fast?" Aaron chuckled, shaking his head.

"Pretty much," Katie said, laughing with Aaron, as she followed him down the ladder.

"I've already loaded the cart," Darius informed the children. "When you have eaten, you can all come with me to the market to set up my stall."

"I'm all ready to go! Come on, everybody!" Peter stood at the gate, shoving in and swallowing the last of the crusty flatbread that had been laid out for him.

"Hold on there a minute," Matthew said, chewing and swallowing as fast as he could. "We're coming, we're coming."

They all trooped out of the courtyard, eased the cart into the street, and headed for the city gates.

Arriving at the market, Darius rolled the cart to a stop in front of his stall. "Leah, Aaron, please unload everything and begin setting up," Darius suggested. "Katie, Matthew, and Peter, perhaps you could help them."

The area just outside the city gates was always filled with lively confusion. This morning, however, there was an unusual amount of turmoil and anxiety. Rippling through the crowd came the shocking news: Laban was dead!

Darius could not believe what he was hearing. How could it be true? Only last evening, Laban had been very much alive. In his mind, Darius could still hear Laban's loud voice bellowing his order that Nephi and his brothers be killed. And now Laban was the one who had lost his life?

"Is it true?" Darius asked the merchant in the stall next to his. "Laban is dead?"

"Yes, it is true!" the man replied.

"But how?"

"He was found dead this morning in the street, not far from his own house. His head was cut off."

"Last night I made a delivery to his house. Laban was there, entertaining his guests," Darius said, shaking his head in disbelief.

"Yes," said the neighboring merchant. "I've heard that he was at home early in the evening. But after the evening meal, he went with the elders of the Jews. He left them after drinking quite a bit and then headed home alone."

Astonished, Darius asked, "Who would have done such a thing?"

"I do not know. But one thing I have heard: Laban's chief steward, a man named Zoram, has disappeared. And Laban's sword is nowhere to be found. That doesn't sound very good to me," he clucked in disapproval as he related the dreadful details.

"Do you think Zoram killed Laban?" Darius was dismayed at the thought.

"I do not know what to think." The merchant, too, seemed bewildered. "I am just telling you the facts as I heard them."

Matthew and Katie looked at each other, their eyes wide with realization, for both remembered the story from their scripture reading. They knew it wasn't Zoram that killed Laban, no matter how things might appear.

Laban's servant, Benjamin, walked up to Darius at his stall. "Shalom, Darius," he said. The impact of Laban's death was evident on his face. "Can you believe this? Just yesterday he was here, and now he is gone. Laban was a hard taskmaster, but I never wished this on him."

"And Zoram has disappeared, is that right?" Darius asked Benjamin.

Benjamin pulled him aside and said quietly, "Yes, he is gone. And do you know what else? The records that Lehi's sons wanted yesterday are gone also!"

"What of the gold and silver Lehi's sons brought? Is that gone too?" Darius wanted to know.

"No, it is still in Laban's treasury." Benjamin shook his head in disbelief. "Why would anyone want the records and not the riches?"

"Some things are more precious than riches," Matthew observed quietly, breaking into the conversation as he lifted a sack of nuts from the cart.

Darius, surprised by Matthew's thoughtful insight, smiled to himself. "Matthew, you are exactly right. There are three things contained on those plates that are much more precious than riches: first, there is the word of God that has been revealed since the world began. Second, there is the testimony of the prophets through the ages. And last, there is the genealogy of Lehi's family."

"You had better watch what you say." Benjamin looked pale and fearful as Darius spoke. He glanced nervously about the stall, scanning the faces of anyone who might have overheard Darius speak with such faith. "There are those who would have you meet the same fate as Laban for proclaiming such things." Then, softening his voice, he asked sincerely, "Do you really believe what you said?"

Knowing that his answer could bring persecution upon himself and his family, Darius considered his words. Then his eyes met Benjamin's sincere and searching gaze. Darius, filled with the Spirit, stood a little taller and answered Benjamin with certainty and conviction. "Yes, Benjamin, I believe what I said. With every fiber of my being, I believe."

Clearly moved by Darius's simple declaration, Benjamin replied, "I can see that you do. Thank you for that testimony." Then, putting his hand on

Darius's shoulder, Benjamin assured him, "You need not worry, friend. Your words are safe with me."

A look of profound relief swept over Darius's face. "Thank you," he replied with feeling.

"I must get back to the house," said Benjamin, remembering his responsibilities. "I will be needed there in this difficult time." But before he left, Benjamin turned to Matthew and Darius and said gratefully, "I will never forget the lesson you both taught me today: There is much in life that is more precious than riches. Much more. Shalom."

"Shalom," said Darius and Matthew together, nodding their farewell.

"Do you think he understands how precious those records really are?" Matthew asked Darius, as they watched Benjamin disappear into the crowds.

"I think perhaps he is beginning to," Darius said, slipping his arm around Matthew's shoulder affectionately. "But you, Matthew, you really understand, don't you?"

Matthew looked up at Darius and uttered his heartfelt reply. "Now more than ever."

Chapter Nine

Better That One Man Should Perish

The citizens of Jerusalem thronged the market-place as news of Laban's death spread. At the city gates, groups of people clustered together, anxiously awaiting further news. Minute by minute, the crowds grew larger and the dialogue more intense.

After a few minutes of moving from group to group, Darius said, "Well, children, I must tend to my stall. You never know who might help themselves to some food while I'm away! Aaron and Leah, you can help me there. Katie, Matthew, and Peter, why don't you move through the crowds and see if you can hear more details of Laban's death?"

"All right," Matthew replied, giving Darius an unexpected hug.

Darius said with surprise, "Well, that was nice,

dear boy. It almost seems like you are saying good-bye!"

"Well, we may have to return soon to our parents, and you have been very kind to us," said Matthew.

"Do not go yet!" wailed Leah. "The festival begins tomorrow!"

Katie stepped in to calm her new friend. "We don't want to worry our loved ones back home. But someday, I hope, we will meet again."

"Let that day come soon!" said Leah, giving Katie a quick squeeze.

"Very soon," Katie said with an affectionate smile, as all the children and Darius hugged one another.

"Now run along, children, and learn what you can about Laban's death," instructed Darius kindly.

"Okay, we'll do that," Matthew said resolutely.

"See you soon," Aaron waved as they slipped into the crowd.

"And be careful," Leah called.

"We will," Katie said, waving until their friends were out of sight.

"It's time to go, isn't it?" a forlorn Peter asked, as

the three children from latter days stood huddled together in the crowd.

"Yes, Peter, I'm afraid it is," Matthew replied, taking Peter's hand in his. "We will have to learn more about Laban's death from the scriptures." He looked back toward Darius's stall, but it had disappeared behind the swarming crowd.

Then, offering his free hand to Katie, he asked, "Ready to go, Sis?"

"I'm ready!" Katie answered wistfully, clasping

Matthew's hand in hers. Then, just as she had come to expect, the wind swirled noisily, lifting the children up, away from the busy marketplace, and onto the soft pillows in Grandma's art cottage.

"'And I was led by the Spirit, not knowing beforehand the things which I should do.'" Grandma rocked gently as she read. "'Nevertheless I went forth, and as I came near unto the house of Laban I

beheld a man, and he had fallen to the earth before me, for he was drunken with wine.'"

"Hey, that's Laban!" Peter burst out proudly.

Grandma peered over her spectacles, smiling and a little surprised. "Good guess, Peter! How did you know that?"

"Oh, you know . . . I just . . ." his voice trailed off. He looked to Katie for help.

"Don't stop now, Grandma. We want to hear the rest," Katie encouraged her.

"Oh, yes, let me see . . . where was I? Here we go. It's still Nephi talking. 'And when I came to him I found that it was Laban,'" she continued.

"See! I knew it!" Peter declared. "Sorry, Grandma. Go ahead."

"'And I beheld his sword, and I drew it forth from the sheath thereof. . . . And it came to pass that I was constrained by the Spirit that I should kill Laban.'"

"What?" Peter sat up in complete disbelief. "That can't be right!"

"You are thinking exactly what Nephi was thinking." Grandma read on. "In his heart Nephi said to himself, 'Never at any time have I shed the blood of man. And I shrunk and would that I might not slay him.'"

"No kidding! I would have felt just the same way," Matthew said, feeling compassion for Nephi.

"Most people would have felt that way. But the Spirit spoke to him again," Grandma said. And she continued reading, "'Behold the Lord hath delivered him into thy hands. . . . It is better that one man should perish than that a nation should dwindle and perish in unbelief.'"

"Dwindle? What does that mean?" Peter asked Grandma.

"Does anyone want to take a guess?" Grandma asked.

"I think it means to get smaller or to disappear," Matthew ventured.

"That's right," Grandma confirmed. "So why would it be so important for Nephi to get the plates?"

"Well," Matthew began slowly, as he thought out loud. "Heavenly Father must have known that Lehi's family would never come back to Jerusalem. They would travel to a different continent, and their descendants would create a whole new nation . . ."

Katie picked right up on Matthew's thinking.

"And because they were leaving Jerusalem forever, they needed a record of their family so that they could remember them."

Grandma smiled. "That is one very good reason. How about another?"

"Well, they also needed a record of all that the prophets had taught. And those plates were written by prophets, right?" Matthew added.

"That's right, and do you know what is amazing?" Grandma asked. "Heavenly Father knew that thousands of years later, you and I would need to know those words. We need to remember the words of the prophets and the commandments revealed to them by God, just as Lehi's descendants did."

"There sure is a lot of remembering going on," Peter said.

"If you don't remember the commandments, it might be tricky to obey them," Matthew reminded him.

Grandma was always surprised how much her young grandchildren understood God's ways.

"Grandma, what happened next?" Peter asked, anxious to hear the rest of the story.

"Well, Peter, Nephi obeyed the Lord and killed Laban. Then listen to what he does." Grandma resumed reading Nephi's words. "'I took the garments of Laban and put them upon mine own body; ... and I did gird on his armor about my loins. And after I had done this, I went forth unto the treasury of Laban. And as I went forth towards the treasury of Laban, behold, I saw the servant of Laban who had the keys of the treasury. And I commanded him in the voice of Laban, that he should go with me into the treasury.'"

"Grandma, can't you tell this part in your own words? This is going to take forever! And I just want to know what happens!" Peter simply couldn't stand the suspense any longer.

"All right," Grandma agreed, "on one condition: I want each of you to read the story right from the scriptures before you go to bed tonight."

"It's a deal!" Peter assured her.

"The name of Laban's servant was Zoram," Grandma began.

"Aha! I know that name!" Peter blurted out. "Sorry, Grandma. Keep going. This is getting really exciting."

"Zoram, of course, thought Nephi was Laban, so he took Nephi into the treasury to get the plates. Nephi told Zoram—in Laban's voice—that he was taking the plates to his elder brethren. Zoram thought Laban meant the brethren of the church, so he followed with the plates."

Katie said knowingly, "But since it was really Nephi wearing Laban's clothes, he meant his older brothers, Laman, Lemuel, and Sam, didn't he?"

"Exactly, Katie." Grandma continued, "Well, Laman, Lemuel, and Sam were waiting for Nephi outside the city walls. And when they thought they saw Laban and his chief steward coming toward them, they were terrified, and they started running away. But Nephi called out to them in his own voice, and they realized it wasn't Laban at all. It was their own brother, disguised in Laban's clothing!"

"Zoram must have been shocked to suddenly realize that an imposter was acting like Laban—and that he had fallen for it!" Katie half-giggled at the thought of Nephi's successful charade.

Grandma took a deep breath and pressed on, "Yes, the scriptures say that poor Zoram was terrified and trembling and about to run. But Nephi was not only stronger and bigger than Zoram, he was also filled with the strength of the Lord. He grabbed Zoram and held onto him."

"He didn't hurt him, did he?" Katie asked.

"Not at all. Nephi explained to Zoram how the Lord had commanded them to get the plates, but Laban wouldn't cooperate. He said the Lord had commanded him to kill Laban so that the records could be preserved. Then Nephi swore a special oath to Zoram. He promised Zoram that if he would come with their family into the wilderness, Zoram would be a free man and have a place with them."

"What did Zoram think of all that?" Matthew asked Grandma.

"The scriptures say that Zoram took courage at the things Nephi said. It couldn't have been easy because going with Lehi's family meant leaving his Jerusalem life behind. The Spirit must have worked upon Zoram, for he made a promise to Nephi and his brothers that he would stay with them from that time on."

Grandma opened her scriptures and read the last verses of the chapter. "'And it came to pass that when Zoram had made an oath unto us, our fears did cease concerning him. And it came to pass that we took the plates of brass and the servant of Laban, and departed into the wilderness, and journeyed unto the tent of our father.'"

Chapter Ten

Lessons Learned

"It sure gives you a lot to think about, doesn't it?" Katie sighed, thoughts of Jerusalem and Laban and Nephi swirling around in her head.

"Amazing how you can go to the same place twice, but learn totally different things the second time," Matthew observed thoughtfully.

Grandma was puzzled. "Where have you been twice?" she asked.

"Jerusalem, of course," Matthew replied matter-of-factly.

"You've been there twice? I didn't know you'd been there even once," Grandma said, looking down at him over her glasses.

"He's just remembering both of your paintings of Jerusalem," Katie explained, smiling up at Grandma innocently.

"Yup, that's exactly what I mean!" Matthew recovered quickly.

"Well, why don't you each tell me one thing you've learned today," Grandma said. "Katie, you start."

"Okay, here's one," Katie began thoughtfully. "When you try to do as Heavenly Father asks, He'll make a way for you to get it done, just like He did for Nephi."

"Yes, I've found that to be true in my own life," Grandma agreed. "As Nephi said, He will 'prepare a way' for you to fulfill His commands. Matthew, what about you?"

Matthew fingered his journal as he replied, "I learned how important it is to keep records."

"What kind of records?" Grandma pressed him.

"Well, there are all kinds of records, but there are some very special records I learned about today," Matthew responded.

"I'm listening," Grandma said with interest. "Go on."

"Well, there are records like the scriptures that tell us the word of God as it was revealed to the prophets. And these records tell what happened when people listened and obeyed and what happened when they didn't. They also record the testimony of those prophets—they're a special witness of what is true. And then there are family records that tell who your ancestors were and what they did long before you were born."

"That's impressive, Matthew. You've learned a lot in just one day," Grandma said with admiration.

Peter waved his arm wildly. "Yeah, someday my kids, or their kids, or their kids' kids, might want to know all about me," Peter pointed out proudly.

"Yes, and I'm sure you'll have a lot to tell, won't you, dear?" Grandma said, a smile creeping over her face.

"Grandma, that's why you gave us these journals, isn't it?" Katie said, lying on her stomach with her journal propped up on the pillow in front of her. In one hand her chin was nestled, and in the other was her pen, poised in the air as she gathered her thoughts.

"That's right, my dear. Do you all know what you're going to write about today?" Grandma quizzed them.

"I do!" Peter piped up. "I'm going to tell anyone who reads my journal that I'd much rather be a Nephi than a Laman or a Lemuel. So I'm going to write about weeds and lemonade, and how important it is to have a good attitude and not to complain."

"I'd say you learned a lot today, too, my dear boy. And what a good lesson to learn, especially in your youth! You'll be a great man one day if you keep thinking like that," Grandma said.

Matthew's pen flashed across the pages of his journal as he furiously recorded his impressions of the day. He paused, sighed loudly, and then resumed writing with increased intensity.

"It looks like you have a lot to say today, Matthew. Are you going to share it with us?" Grandma asked. Matthew, not hearing a word she said, kept right on writing. "Matthew?" Grandma spoke louder this time.

"What?" Startled, Matthew looked up from his journal. "What did you say, Grandma?"

Grandma repeated her question. "I just wondered if you were going to share what you are writing in your journal."

"Yes, I have a surprise for all of you, but you'll have to give me a few more minutes to finish it." He buried his nose in his journal and continued writing.

"I can hardly wait," Grandma said to Katie and Peter.

"Grandma, did you keep a journal?" Katie asked.

"Yes and no. At certain times I have written more than at other times. I'm still learning, too! Do you want to hear an entry from my journal?" Grandma asked.

"Oh, yes, please," Katie and Peter answered in unison. Matthew was still completely preoccupied with his writing.

"Let's see, where is that entry?" Grandma said, flipping through her journal to find her place. "Oh, here it is. I wrote this just after you were here last time." She slipped on her reading glasses, adjusted them, and began reading. "My grandchildren, Katie, Matthew, and Peter, have just left. What a blessing they are in my life! When I am with them I feel young again, and I rediscover the world through their eyes. I hope they are learning something from me, too. I am so grateful to share with them the treasures I've found in the scriptures. I am looking forward to their next visit already. I had better get busy on another painting so we can get together soon."

"Grandma, you must have looked at my journal

entry," Katie said in wonderment. "Listen to this: 'Grandma doesn't seem old to me at all. She loves to hear what I'm thinking, and I love to hear what she is thinking, too. She is my best friend. I hope she finishes her next painting so that we can come back soon.'" Katie smiled up at Grandma.

"Listen to what I wrote!" Peter jumped up and planted a big kiss on Grandma's cheek. "'I love my Grandma! She is totally cool! And she knows a lot, too. She's taught me a lot about the scriptures—and I'm having a great time learning!' Just think, when my kids read this journal, they'll know how much I loved my family, and they'll know how much I loved the scriptures. Then maybe they'll want to have those things in their lives, too!"

"I hope so, Peter. I really hope so," Grandma said.

"I'm finished!" Matthew announced proudly, waving his journal in the air. "I've done something totally different this time! I've written a song about what I've learned. Do you want to hear it?"

"You'd better believe it!" Katie cried, clapping her hands together. "This is the first time you've shared your songs with anyone."

"I know," Matthew said sheepishly, "but this is

one I want to share." He retrieved Grandma's old guitar from the corner of the studio. As he plucked each string in turn and twisted the tuning pegs, Grandma, Katie, and Peter curled up together on the pillows, awaiting Matthew's performance.

While he adjusted the pegs, Matthew explained, "Now, remember, I'm just learning to play the guitar. So I wrote this song to a melody I already knew. And the chords are real basic . . ."

"Okay, okay. Don't worry, Matthew. We'll love it no matter what!" Katie was growing impatient.

With the guitar nicely tuned, Matthew strummed the first chord tentatively, and began singing:

In ages now long past and gone,
The prophets on the earth
Wrote down the truths revealed by God,
Words of eternal worth.
Oh, records, records, written records
Kept for us today
Are now the scriptures helping us
Remember and obey.

In ages that are yet to come,
No one will still be here
Who knew the prophets of today
And heard their message clear.

Oh, records, records, written records
That we keep today
Will help God's children yet to live
Remember and obey.

Someday I know I'll leave the earth,
And no one will be here
Who knew the feelings of my heart,
The things that I hold dear.
Oh, records, records, written records
I will write each day
For I hope my descendants will
Remember and obey.

About the Authors

Alice W. Johnson, a published author and composer, is a featured speaker for youth groups, adult firesides, and women's seminars. A former executive in a worldwide strategy consulting company, and then in a leadership training firm, Alice is now a homemaker living in Eagle, Idaho, with her husband and their four young children.

Allison H. Warner gained her early experience living with her family in countries around the world. Returning to the United States as a young woman, she began her vocation as an actress and writer, developing and performing in such productions as *The Farley Family Reunion*. She and her husband reside in Provo, Utah, where they are raising two active boys.

About the Illustrator

Jerry Harston held a degree in graphic design and illustrated more than thirty children's books. He received many honors for his art, and his clients included numerous Fortune 500 corporations. Jerry passed away in December 2009.